HISTORY THROUGH SOURCES

The
Reformation

RIGBY INTERACTIVE LIBRARY

Michael Mullett

RIGBY
INTERACTIVE
LIBRARY

Printed in Hong Kong

00 99 98 97 96
10 9 8 7 6 5 4 3 2 1

Library of Congress Cataloging-in-Publication Data
Mullett, Michael A.
The Reformation/Michael Mullett.
p. cm. — (History through sources—Rigby Interactive library)
Includes index.
Summary: History of the Reformation and the Counter Reformation in the sixteenth century.
ISBN 1-57572-011-6 (lib. bdg.)
1. Reformation—Juvenile literature. [1. Christianity—History.] I. Title. II. Series.
BR308.M85   1996
270.6—dc20
95-36151
CIP
AC

Designed by Ron Kamen, Green Door Design

Produced by AMR

Illustrated by Jeff Edwards

Acknowledgments

The author and publisher would like to thank the following for permission to reproduce photographs:

Ace Photo Agency: p.44
Agenzia Giornalistica Italia SpA: p.41
AKG London: p.19
Ann Ronan Picture Library: p.14
Archiv für Kunst und Geschichte: p.32
Art & Architecture Collection: p.34
British Library: p.9, p.26
Eigentum des Germanischen National Museums: p.8
E. T. Archive: p.40
Fotoatelier Gerhard Howald: p.6
Museo Thyssen-Bornemisza: p.24
Photo R. M. N.: p.7, p.36
Rafael Macia: p.44
Statens Konstmuseer, Stockholm: p.18
The Bridgeman Art Library: p.29
The Mansell Collection: p.11, p.21

Cover photograph reproduced with permission of Giraudon.

The author and publisher would also like to thank Dr. Thomas Brady of the University of California, Berkeley, for his comments in the preparation of this book.

Every effort has been made to contact copyright holders of material published in this book. Any omissions will be rectified in subsequent printings if notice is given to the publisher.

To Gerard, Rhiannon and James, with love from Dad.

Details of Written Sources

Sources in this book are both primary and secondary. *Primary sources* are texts, eyewitness accounts, quotations, photographs, or artwork that date from the historical period. *Secondary sources* are analyses by experts in the field. In some cases, the wording and sentence structure of sources have been simplified to ensure that they are accessible to students.

G. R. Elton (ed.), *Renaissance and Reformation: 1300–1648*, Collier-Macmillan, 1963: 1.1, 1.2, 3.6, 4.4
Nevill Coghill (ed.), *Chaucer: The Canterbury Tales*, Penguin Classics: 1.3
Ian D. Kingston Siggins, *Luther*, Oliver & Boyd, 1972: 2.1
Michael Mullett, *Luther*, Routledge, Lancaster Pamphlets, 1986: 2.2, 2.3
Hans J. Hillerbrand, *The Reformation in Its Own Words*, SCM Press, 1964: 2.4, 2.5, 3.2, 3.3, 3.4, 3.5, 4.3, 4.7
B. J. Kidd, *Documents of the Continental Reformation*, Clarendon Press, 1911: 3.1
C. R. N. Routh, *They Saw It Happen in Europe: An Anthology of Eyewitness Accounts of Events in European History 1450–1660*, Basil Blackwell, 1965: 4.1, 4.2
J. H. Parry (ed.), *The European Renaissance: Selected Documents*, Macmillan, 1968: 4.5
David B. Quinn (ed.), *North American Discovery Circa 1000–1612*, Harper & Row, 1971: 4.6
Donald Weinstein (ed.), *The Renaissance and the Reformation: 1300–1600*, The Free Press, 1965: 5.1, 5.2

Note to the Reader

In this book some words are printed in **bold** type. This indicates that the word is listed in the glossary on pages 46–47. The glossary gives a brief explanation of words that may be new to you.

Contents

The State of the Catholic Church

Criticism of the Church

Many criticisms were made of the Catholic Church in Europe up to and including the 16th century. Many people were saying that the Catholic Church was rotten and corrupt, that its leaders were involved in wars and were crazy for money. They said that in the beginning, Jesus Christ and His followers, the Apostles, had founded a pure Christian Church, but that it had become spoiled. They demanded that the Church be taken back to the way Christ had left it.

The Call for Reform

Some Church leaders also criticized the Catholic Church and tried to remedy its faults. In 1537, leaders of the Catholic Church attacked priests who thought only about money. They also denounced priests who said religious services carelessly. They were also upset that, in Rome, prostitutes were tolerated by Church leaders.

JOHN HUS

John Hus (1369–1415) was born in Bohemia, in eastern Europe, and came from a peasant background. He studied at the University of Prague, where he became rector. He was an excellent preacher, very popular with the people of Prague. Hus made deep criticisms of the state of the Church, including its simony. He was accused of **heresy**, or undermining the beliefs of the Church, and was executed by burning in 1415.

SOURCE 1

May the Lord grant that the present Pope and his successors stop meddling in wars and give no church positions to unworthy men for money, but follow Christ! But it seems to me that few of them will be willing to enter upon the way of Christ, the way of humility, poverty, and of hard work. Worldly possessions have blocked the way of Christ and priests are obsessed with greed for money and with quarrels.

*John Hus wrote these criticisms of the Church in a book called **On Simony** (1413). **Simony** is the selling of holy objects and positions in the Church for money.*

SOURCE 2

In this very city of Rome prostitutes walk openly as if they were respectable married women. Noblemen who are close friends of **cardinals** and priests go with them openly.

*This source is from a list of criticisms made by Church leaders in 1537, called **Advice on the Reform of the Church**. The leaders thought of Rome, the headquarters of the Church, as a special, holy city that had become polluted.*

Rome

Rome was the headquarters of the pope. Catholics believed that the pope ruled the Church as deputy for Christ. But in about the year 1500, popes gave a bad example to Christians and were totally unlike Christ.

These cartoons are from a German work of 1521. The artists show contrasts between Christ, who is shown as a humble and suffering servant, and the Pope, who is shown as a proud tyrant.

Alexander VI

One of these corrupt popes was Alexander VI, who was pope from 1492 to 1503. Alexander paid huge bribes to become pope. Although priests, bishops, and popes were not supposed to have sexual relationships, Alexander had sons and daughters. He used his position as pope to benefit his family, especially his son Cesare Borgia.

The Cardinals

At the top levels of government in the Catholic Church, the cardinals helped the pope to rule. They chose the pope from among themselves. Most of the cardinals thought more about their families, money, and politics than they thought about following Christ and teaching ordinary people about Him.

*This early 16th-century cartoon, showing an imaginary scene, is an example of **anticlericalism,** a hatred of priests and church leaders. Anticlericalism was caused by the greed and arrogance of many Churchmen.*

The Church: What Was Wrong

In their *Advice on the Reform of the Church*, Church leaders say:

- "Christ's Church is fallen, and almost collapsed."
- Unworthy, ignorant, immoral men are made priests, for money.
- Bishops cannot control or discipline their priests.
- Wrong ideas are taught in the universities.
- Everything is sold for money.
- Rome gives a bad example to the whole Christian world.

The Bishops

Many bishops spent most of their time working for kings and rulers and little time doing their work of encouraging priests to look after the religious needs of the people.

Priests, Monks and Friars

Priests

Priests took care of parishes. Many priests did not have a true inner calling, or vocation, to be devoted and hard-working. To make enough money, some priests had to take care of two or more parishes and could not care for one village properly.

Monks

Monks were supposed to live simply. This meant that they were to eat and drink only enough for their health, to pray together to God in their monasteries, to work in the fields and grow their food, and to study regularly. But by 1500 many monks had big incomes, ate and drank richly, and employed servants to do their work.

Friars

Besides many priests and monks, there were also thousands of **friars**. These men were supposed to live in poverty, like Christ, and to teach the ordinary people about Him. But many friars lived only for money and pleasure.

Superstition

Many priests, monks, and friars tried to make money by taking advantage of the religious beliefs of ordinary people. People believed that they could please God and have their sins forgiven if they paid to visit relics, which were parts of bodies or clothing of dead holy people.

This early 16th-century German cartoon shows some people's hatred of monks. The monk is shown as a wolf devouring Christians, who are shown as defenseless sheep.

Some of these relics were fakes. One church claimed to have the head of St. John the Baptist, Christ's holy cousin. Another said it had straw from the stable where Christ was born, and another claimed it had milk from Christ's mother, Mary.

SOURCE 3

He kept his hood stuffed with pins for curls,
And pocket-knives, to give to pretty girls.
He knew the taverns well in every town,
And every innkeeper and barmaid too.

*In his **Canterbury Tales** (1387), the English poet Geoffrey Chaucer (1340–1400) described a merry friar who loved women and drinking. Most of Chaucer's readers would have known of a friar like this.*

Confession and Indulgences

At least once a year, people were supposed to **confess** their sins, such as murder, violence, or having sexual relations outside of marriage, to their priest. People believed that if they confessed everything and were truly sorry, and if they accepted punishment for what they had done by saying prayers or doing good deeds, they were forgiven. Then, when they died, their souls went into a temporary state called **purgatory**, where they were punished to purify them from sin.

The Catholic Church granted **indulgences** to release people from all or part of their punishment. Originally, indulgences could be given for doing good and holy deeds, or by donating money to the Church. But by 1500 indulgences were sometimes sold. Sometimes people were told they could buy indulgences to keep themselves and their families out of purgatory.

Christian Humanists

Humanists were people who wanted to return to ideas found in old Greek and Latin writings of Greece and Rome, written many centuries earlier. Christian Humanists also wanted to get back to these ideas, but they were mainly concerned with learning about the early Christian Church, before it had become involved with money-making and superstition. They wanted to read the books of the early Church, especially the gospels of Christ, in the original language of Greek, so that they would know exactly what the writings meant. The leader of the Christian Humanists was Desiderius Erasmus (1466–1536), who attacked superstitions in the Catholic Church in his writing.

One of Eramus's most important tasks was to publish the *New Testament*, in its original language, Greek, which he did in 1516. It contained the gospels of Christ and other important early Christian writings, including the letters of the Apostle St. Paul. His version of the New Testament was used for printed translations into the ordinary languages of European people.

Erasmus painted by Hans Holbein the Younger (1497–1543) in 1532.

Martin Luther and the German Reformation

Martin Luther

Martin Luther was born in the heart of Germany in 1483. His mother and father came from peasant backgrounds. They were hard-working people, and Martin's father, Hans, became a successful mine operator. The Luthers made enough money to send their son, Martin, to good schools. They planned for him to become a successful lawyer who would look after them in their old age.

Young Luther

Martin Luther did not want that kind of success. He was very religious. Like many other people of his time, he worried about whether or not God was pleased with him or whether God would punish him for his sins in hell or purgatory.

Anxiety

A friend of Luther died of a plague, and Luther worried about the possibility that he might also suddenly die. He decided to give the rest of his life to trying to please God and keep God's anger away. He had to stand up to his father and disobey his orders that he become a lawyer.

Luther Becomes a Monk

Luther did not join one of the monasteries where monks lived comfortably. He joined a strict monastery, in the German town of Erfurt, in 1505.

Luther was a good monk. He also became a university teacher. He worked very hard, prayed to God, lived very simply, and went to confession often.

But living as a monk did not satisfy Luther. He felt God was angry with him and would send him to hell for his sins. He was

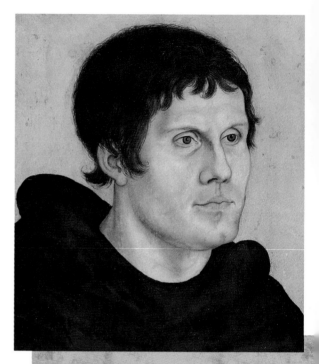

The German artist Lucas Cranach the Elder (1472–1553) painted Luther as a monk, showing how serious Luther was (1520).

puzzled and unhappy. He was suffering from deep depression and anxiety.

Luther Finds a Way Out

Luther's counselor in the monastery was a well-known religious adviser in Germany, Johann von Staupitz (1468–1525). Staupitz advised Luther to read the Bible carefully.

Luther and St. Paul

In the Bible, Luther read a passage in the letter of St. Paul to the early Christians in Rome. St. Paul wrote that all Christians had to do was have faith that Christ had died on the cross to save them. Luther eventually found an amazing relief in this passage. God, instead of being an angry judge, was a kind and loving Father.

St. Paul's Letter

In his letter "to the Romans", St. Paul wrote that Christians were forgiven by God, without any effort on their part, because they believed that Christ had died for them. This made such things as indulgences useless. Yet in 1517 indulgences were being sold in Luther's neighborhood by a friar named Johann Tetzel. Tetzel used false promises to sell his indulgences.

SOURCE 1

I was a monk without any complaint. I kept all my monk's vows and promises as well as I could, night and day. I prayed and I prayed—and I certainly had no wife! In fact, you never saw such a monk as I was. And yet I felt no real peace of mind in doing my duty so well.

All the time I was so sad and worried that God was not kind to me. I often went to Confession. Yet once when I went to Confession, the priest said to me, "God isn't angry with you—you're angry with Him." There was a lot of truth in that.

*These words of Luther's are put together from lectures he gave at the university and from his later **Table Talk** (1566), when Luther was talking to his family and friends over the dinner table.*

Martin Luther becomes a Reformer

Luther's Attitude

What really bothered Luther was not Tetzel's methods, but what indulgences taught people about themselves and God. Indulgences made them think that they could buy their way into God's favor. Luther condemned such views in his *Ninety-Five Theses* of November 1517. These were quickly printed, and they caused a storm because indulgences were given out by the Pope.

Luther and the Pope

Luther was calling the Pope's power in question. In 1518 and 1519 the Pope's men tried hard to get Luther to change his mind. He refused. In 1520 Pope Leo X condemned Luther. When Luther refused to give in, the Pope expelled him from the Church.

Bulla contra errores Martini Lutheri et sequacium.

*The cover of the Pope's document condemning Luther. The title of the Pope's letter, or **bull**, was, in Latin, **Exsurge Domine**, or "Rise Up Lord God". It called Luther a wild boar in God's vineyard.*

Luther in Trouble

Luther at this time was busy writing and publishing his books. In one book, in 1520, he called for the social reform of Germany. In another one he said that Christ has made all His followers free. In another he attacked the Pope as the enemy of Christ.

To attack the Pope was highly dangerous because the government and the Church were closely linked. Germany had many local rulers, but above them all was the Holy Roman Emperor, Charles V, a strong Catholic.

Luther at the Diet of Worms

In 1521, Luther had to come before the Emperor Charles and the German Diet, or Parliament, meeting in the city of Worms. Here Luther was asked to give up his religious ideas. He replied that he could not.

Luther was now officially a heretic, an enemy of the Church. He could be burned to death, as John Hus had been. But his local ruler, Elector Frederick, had him secretly taken to a remote castle, where Luther lived in disguise under a false name.

Luther and the Bible

Luther loved the Bible. He said he was "captive" to it. In his castle hideaway, he started to work on the huge job of translating the entire Bible into German. In 1522, he returned to Wittenberg to take control of a reform group that was making changes in the way people worshipped God.

Luther Settles Down

In 1524, Luther married a former nun, Katherina von Bora, and settled down to raise a family. He spent the rest of his life teaching, writing, and organizing religious changes in his part of Germany. He was officially an outlaw, so he could not travel far. He worked incredibly hard. The modern American version of his writings runs to more than 50 thick volumes.

Luther was a kind, warm-hearted man. But he attacked anyone he felt was an enemy of Christ. The worst side of him was expressed in his attacks on Jews. He also attacked Turks, who were Muslims, Catholic followers of the Pope, and even other groups of Protestants. These attacks became more and more violent as he grew older.

SOURCE 2

Luther was asked to give up his ideas contained in his writings. He answered: "Your majesty the Emperor and the members of the Diet have asked for a simple answer. Here it is: Unless I am convinced by the Bible or by good arguments, I must be true to my conscience, which is rooted in the Bible. So I **cannot** give up, because it's dangerous to go against your conscience. God help me. Amen."

These were Luther's words at the Diet of Worms. They are very brave words, because Luther knew that he was disobeying the Church and the government, and that most others who had done this were burned to death.

Following his outburst against the Church, Luther had to become closely involved with German politics. He had disobeyed the Emperor, and he needed his own ruler's protection. He wrote about Germany's problems.

Luther and the Peasants

Luther was born into a peasant family. He said: "I am a peasant's son; my father, grandfather, and ancestors have all been just peasants." He knew the peasants were badly treated. He criticized the landlords and rulers of Germany for over-taxing the peasants and putting too many demands on them.

Luther and Germany's Problems

Germany at the beginning of the 16th century had many difficulties.

- Too many governments. As well as big states, like Saxony where Luther lived, Germany had too many tiny states and cities that governed themselves.

- Weak federal government. The official overlord of Germany, The Holy Roman Emperor, did not have enough power to rule Germany properly.

- Discontent. Germans believed that their money was going out of the country, to Rome. Many demanded reform in the country's government. Most Germans were peasants. Some of them were doing well, but most were worse off than they had been. Germany was on the edge of an explosion.

This picture of a peasant rebel is from a pamphlet by the writer Pamphilus Gengenbach. The peasant is shown with a huge boot, the symbol of the rising.

In Luther's lifetime, Germany's population of peasants was rising sharply. Landlords knew there were too many peasants wanting to rent farms. They could demand high rents and taxes and get unpaid farm work from peasants. There were many small revolts of unhappy peasants around Germany at this time.

Luther, Germany and the Peasants' Revolt

In 1525, revolts in German regions joined together in one great uprising by the peasants. It is sometimes called the "Peasants' War."

This contemporary illustration shows German peasants getting ready for revolt in 1525. Many of the peasants were well armed, with swords and armor.

The Peasants' Manifesto

The peasants issued a **manifesto**, a list of their problems and complaints, called *The Twelve Articles of Memmingen* (1525). It had some of Luther's ideas about the way Christians were free. Luther said that the peasants' complaints about high taxes and payments were "fair and just". But when the peasants used violence, Luther was disgusted. In 1525, in his work *Against the Murdering, Thieving Hordes of Peasants*, he called on the rulers to kill all the rebels. The peasant rebellion was put down with great cruelty.

The Peasants' Failure

The peasants began with a moderate program and image. In *The Twelve Articles of Memmingen*, they tried to appeal to broad German opinion. But some peasants got drunk, and they raped and plundered. In battle the peasants were no match for the armies of the rulers, with their well-trained cavalry. The peasants felt that Luther had let them down.

The Spread of Luther's Ideas

Luther knew how useful the printing press was to him. While he stayed in Wittenberg, his ideas traveled around the country in thousands of printed copies of his books. People who could read would read Luther's writings to others in public places. Some priests read Luther's writings and then put his ideas into their sermons. In these ways Luther's religious ideas were spread, especially in cities.

Most of Germany's important cities ruled themselves through their city councils and could choose their religion. By 1525, one of Germany's most important cities, Nuremberg, decided to become Lutheran. Nuremberg was followed by other important cities, such as Strassburg (now Strasbourg in France) and Augsburg. Soon, about two-thirds of the important cities in the German regions left the Catholic Church.

The German states were ruled by their princes. In the 1520s and 1530s, several of these princes decided to bring Luther's ideas into their states and leave the Catholic Church, becoming **Protestant**. The Holy Roman Emperor Charles V tried to stop this. Civil war broke out. In the *Peace of Augsburg* of 1555, the German states and cities were left to decide whether they wanted to be Catholic or Lutheran.

The Twelve Articles of Memmingen

The peasants' demands include:

- The right to elect their priests.
- Agreed payments to priests.
- An end to peasant slavery and to death taxes.
- Free hunting, fishing, and access to woodland.
- Fair rents.
- No new laws against the peasants.
- The return of common fields.

SOURCE 3

The peasants are rash rebels. The lords are God's punishment on them. A rebel doesn't deserve to be answered with reason, but only with a fist in the mouth.

*In these words from his pamphlet **Against the Murdering, Thieving Hordes of Peasants** (1525), Luther condemned the peasant rebels.*

MARTIN LUTHER

The ideas of Martin Luther (1483–1546) changed the Church and brought in the Reformation, the huge movement that broke from the Catholic Church in the 16th century, creating new Protestant Churches. Services were to be simpler and held in the language of the people, not the Latin of the Catholic service. Priests could marry. There would be no monks. Church wealth should go to the community. After many years of very hard work, Luther died in 1546. His ideas brought about huge changes.

Anabaptists

Although Luther and his followers made enormous changes, there were those who felt the reforms did not go far enough. One of the groups of people who believed that the reforms did not go far enough was that of the **Anabaptists**.

Anabaptists can be divided into two kinds: peaceful Anabaptists, and violent, or revolutionary, Anabaptists. The peaceful Anabaptists developed into important Christian groups in the United States, such as the **Hutterites** and the **Amish**. These groups live in peace with everyone, work on their farms, and share their property in common.

The Beginnings of the Anabaptists

Switzerland bordered on Germany. Luther's ideas quickly spread there. Led by Huldreich Zwingli (1484–1531), the Swiss city of Zürich brought in the Reformation. Zwingli worked closely with the ruling city council of Zürich and tried to ensure that everyone remained a member of the same church. This was done by **baptizing** all children into the church shortly after their birth to make sure that everyone in the community would also be a member of the same church. It would keep together the church, the state, and the community. However, some people in the Zürich area read in the Bible that the early Christians, whose beliefs they wanted to follow, joined the church as adults, when they knew what they were doing. As believers, they could be baptized as a sign that they were "born again."

SOURCE 4

In order that God's holy work might be made known and revealed to everyone, there developed first in Switzerland an extraordinary awakening and preparation, as follows. Two men saw into the Lord's mind and believed that people must be correctly baptized according to the Christian way of the Lord Himself, since Christ says that whoever believes and is baptized will be saved. Zwingli did not wish this and claimed that a revolt would break out if it was brought in. But we said that God's clear orders could not be ignored for that reason.

*This source is from a sixteenth-century Anabaptist account of the beginnings of the movement, called **The Oldest Chronicle of the Hutterite Brethren**. The Hutterites were an important branch of peaceful Anabaptists. The source is heavily weighted on the side of the Anabaptists.*

Adult Baptism

In 1525, opponents of Zwingli began to baptize adults. They called this "believers' baptism." But it was against the law of Zürich because it would mean people could choose whether or not they wished to be members of the main Church, which the state supported. Zwingli called these people "Anabaptists", meaning people who were baptized again. Some of them were thrown out of Zürich, thus spreading the Anabaptist message into other parts of Switzerland, then into Germany and the Netherlands.

Anabaptism spread from Switzerland into Germany, Austria, and the Netherlands. Anabaptists were harshly persecuted by all sides. They were accused of opposing the government and the Church. They appealed to the poor, peasants, miners, and people employed in making cloth. Their members preached and brought in new members.

What Anabaptists Believed

The Anabaptists made a number of lists of their beliefs so as to give people a clearer understanding of their ideas. One of these lists was the *Schleitheim Articles* of 1527. In it the Anabaptists said that they wanted baptism only for those who were truly sorry for their sins and that true Christians should be apart from the wicked world. Governments, they said, existed mainly to control wicked people. They did not believe that Christians should swear oaths to confirm their statements or to prove their loyalty to the government.

Executions of Anabaptists in the Netherlands, in 1524, from a history of persecution (1685) by the Dutch historian Jans van Braght.

How Were Anabaptists Different?

Anabaptists differed from followers of the Catholic Church and the churches of the Reformation. They:

- Ignored the difference between priests and ordinary people.
- Demanded that people join the Church only as real believers.
- Had simple, basic Christian beliefs based on the Bible.
- Did not believe in a close link between the Church and the government.

The End of the World

The harassment the Anabaptists received for their beliefs made many of them long for a new coming of Christ and the end of the wicked world around them. One of the Anabaptist leaders was Melchior Hoffmann. He predicted that Christ would come again 1500 years after His death on the Cross. That would have been in 1533.

Hoffmann believed that Strassburg, one of the cities that had taken up the Reformation, would be the "new Jerusalem." Some of Hoffmann's followers started to believe that they could hasten the end of the world by their own actions, including violence.

MELCHIOR HOFFMANN

Melchior Hoffmann (1500–1543) was a typical Anabaptist because, although he was a religious leader and teacher, he was not a priest. Like many Anabaptists, he was a craftsman—a furrier. He came from southwest Germany and preached in Sweden, Denmark, and the Netherlands.

In 1529, Hoffmann came to the city of Strassburg. There he had followers who were known as "Melchiorites." They looked forward to the second coming of Christ. Hoffmann said that he was Elijah, a prophet in the Bible. Hoffmann died in prison in Strassburg in 1543, but before he died some of his followers created a revolution in another German city, Münster. This went against the peaceful beliefs of the early Anabaptists. For a while, the Anabaptists seemed to become a terrorist movement.

Revolutionary Anabaptists

Many German cities went over to the Reformation. One of them was Münster, in northwest Germany. Münster was ruled by a Catholic bishop, but when the city gave up the Catholic religion in 1533, the bishop was thrown out.

Münster, the City of God

The followers of Melchior Hoffmann began to believe that Münster, not Strassburg, was God's special chosen city. Many Anabaptists traveled to Münster from the Netherlands. Anabaptists took over the city government and won elections to the city council in 1534. Baptism of children was ended, and baptism of adults was introduced. The supporters of the Catholic bishop of Münster surrounded the city in a **siege**.

Jan Matthijs

Jan Matthijs was a baker from the Netherlands and a close follower of Hoffmann. He became ruler of Münster and stopped people from having personal possessions. Everyone had to share, because food was scarce during the siege. In May 1534, Matthijs was killed leading his men against the siege. The next leader was Jan Beukels.

Beukels made himself King of Münster. He brought in polygamy, a way of life in which all men had several wives. He himself had 15. Meanwhile, people were starving in the siege and were eating worms and slugs. In 1535 Münster gave up the fight, and the bishop came back.

SOURCE 5

Beukels was the first to take a second wife. Then he continued to take more wives until he had fifteen. All the Netherlanders in Münster and all the real Anabaptists there had extra wives. In fact, they forced their first wives to go and get second wives for them. The devil had a good laugh at all this. Those who had old wives and wanted young ones got what they wished.

A spy got in and reported that Beukels rode around town on a fine horse which was covered in black–green velvet. Beukels wore a golden crown on his head and held a gold rod in his hand. A robe made up with gold with two swords hung from his neck. In every way he acted like a king. He didn't trust his subjects and used informers to keep a close watch on them.

Food is very scarce. Nearly all the cats and dogs have been eaten. Most people eat roots and grasses. A miller said he scraped the white stuff off the walls, mixed it with water, and gave it to his children to drink. Twenty-five horses have been eaten, cats are roasted on spears, and mice are cooked in pans.

> These are some of the reports written about Münster in 1535. They come from 16th-century German reports. The reports were written by enemies of the Anabaptists. Their writings mocked Beukels and the Anabaptists.

The Fall of Münster

Before the Anabaptists in Münster gave up, they were promised fair terms. These terms were swept aside when the bishop came back. Hundreds of Anabaptists in the city were killed. Beukels was tortured to death with red-hot pincers. The rulers linked all Anabaptists to the events that had taken place in Münster. Thousands more Anabaptists were now put to death because they were all blamed for what had happened in Münster.

But what happened in Münster was not typical of the way Anabaptism had started out. The first Anabaptists believed in baptism for true followers of Christ, but they did not believe in forcing people into baptism, as happened in Münster. Many Anabaptists believed in sharing property, as the early Christians had done, but they did not agree with forcing people to give up their goods.

Menno Simmons

Menno Simmons thought that what happened in Münster had led the Anabaptist movement in the wrong direction. He made it his job to bring back a true form of Anabaptism, which would be brotherly, non-violent, and simple.

Under the leadership of people like Menno Simmons, the Anabaptist movement went back to its true, peaceful nature. Some groups, such as the Hutterites, lived in farming communities, sharing everything they produced. Groups such as these live peacefully in the United States and Canada today.

Simmons then taught Anabaptist groups. In 1540 he published a book called *Fondamentboek*, or "Book of Basics", explaining his type of Anabaptism. He stressed that violence had to be avoided by Christians.

A Hutterite Anabaptist family in front of a house for several families. Hutterite Anabaptists live and work together, without private property.

MENNO SIMMONS

Menno Simmons (1491–1561) was a Catholic priest from the town of Witmarsum in the Netherlands. He began his work as a village priest in 1524, but he soon began have doubts about the Catholic services. He read Luther's writings and the Bible and became sure that baptizing babies was wrong. He stopped being a Catholic priest in 1536.

The Spread of Reformation

Scandinavia and Switzerland

Scandinavia is the name for a group of countries in northern Europe, including Norway, Denmark, and Sweden. In these kingdoms, bringing in the Reformation involved political and money issues. These included the power of the king in his kingdom, the freedom of the nation from having churches ruled by people in Rome, and the distribution of the property of the Church.

Denmark

In southern Scandinavia, near Denmark's border with Germany, the Lutheran Hermann Tast (1490–1551) was preaching in the early 1520s. Lutheran Hans Tausen (1494–1561) was preaching in the north. Between 1523 and 1559, the Danish Kings Fredrik I and Christian II protected the preachers and introduced the Reformation with the backing of the lords and the parliament.

Sweden

In the main city of Sweden, Stockholm, German merchants spread Luther's ideas. From 1527, King Gustavus Vasa (1496–1560), brought in the Reformation. He gave his backing to the leading Swedish follower of Luther, Olav Pedersson (1493–1552).

The Reformation in Scandinavia

The Reformation was also brought to other parts of Scandinavia—Finland, Iceland, and Norway. Monasteries were closed down, and Bibles and service books were issued in the language of the people.

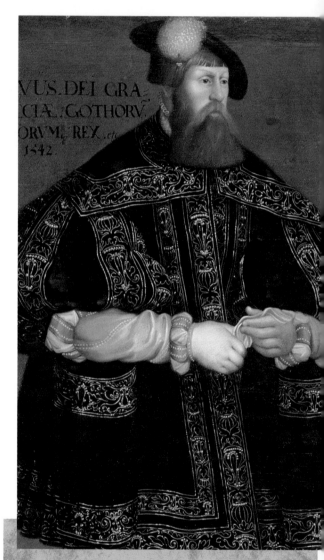

This painting of Gustavus Vasa is anonymous and dates from 1542. It shows him at the age of 46, splendidly dressed and kingly. Gustavus was one of a number of powerful northern European rulers who used their power to bring about religious change.

GUSTAVUS VASA

Gustavus Vasa (1496–1560), a Swedish nobleman, took part in his country's struggle for freedom from Denmark in 1518. He was taken prisoner, but he escaped and became a fugitive. In 1520, the Danes massacred Swedes in Stockholm, and Sweden was furious. Gustavus led the resistance and captured Stockholm from the Danes in 1523, freeing his country. Gustavus was elected king and began to bring in the Reformation.

SOURCE 1

In June 1524, the council of Zürich ordered that there should be no more playing of church organs in the city; no ringing of bells for the dead or for good weather; no more blessing of salt, water, and candles; but that all such superstitions should cease and be done away with entirely, because they are all against the clear word of God.

This is an order of the Zürich city council, carefully written down to record the progress of the Reformation in the city. The council acted on Zwingli's ideas for a simpler way of worshiping God.

Switzerland

Like Scandinavia, Switzerland was open to ideas from its neighbor, Germany. The most important Swiss reformer, Huldreich Zwingli of Zürich (1484–1531), studied Luther's books. He said: "I have not learned the teachings of Christ from Luther but from the word of God itself." Zwingli also took many of his ideas from Erasmus. He became the preacher at the main church in Zürich in 1518, and in the 1520s he brought in the Reformation with the support of the city council. Zwingli made Church worship even simpler than Luther had.

Other Swiss cities such as Bern and Basel also brought in the Reformation. Before Luther died, the Reformation had spread very far, and some forms that it took had moved quite a long way from Luther's original ideas.

Huldreich Zwingli was one of a number of **civic** religious reformers. They worked closely with city councils to bring in religious changes, such as making the services simpler and putting them in the language of the ordinary people. Another civic reformer was Martin Bucer (1491-1551), who set up the Reformation in the German city of Strassburg.

The painting of Huldreich Zwingli is by a Swiss artist, Hans Asper. It was made in 1531, the year of Zwingli's death.

Cities and the Reformation

Cities, especially in Germany and Switzerland, were often quick to take up the Reformation. Religious change often allowed them to free themselves from the rule of a Catholic bishop. City governments could increase their power by introducing the Reformation and controlling the new Church organization.

Towns and Change

Townspeople themselves were eager for change and experiment. From their point of view, Catholicism was tied in with customs and festivals that made sense in a farming community. People in towns and cities needed to have their industries work without being interrupted by all the feast days of the Catholic faith.

The Reformation was also linked to education, reading, and literacy. There were more schools in towns than in the country, and more townspeople than peasants could read. Towns and cities had printing presses that spread Protestant ideas. The towns and cities of Europe were the nerve centers of the Reformation.

John Calvin

John Calvin was born in the town of Noyon, in northeastern France, in 1509. His father was a lawyer who worked for the Church. Calvin's father planned that John would go to a university, become a priest, and get rich and famous.

Calvin went to a university in Paris, where he studied Latin, and to the Universities of Orléans and Bourges, where he studied Greek and law as well as religion. He published an important book about an ancient Roman thinker, Seneca.

Calvin Converted

In the early 1530s, Calvin was won over, or **converted**, to Reformation ideas, leaving the Catholic Church. He became a member of a small group of Protestants, or people who wanted the Reformation. One of them was the rector, or head, of the university in Paris, Nicholas Cop. When he became head of the university, Cop made a speech that many people thought attacked the Catholic Church. Calvin may have helped him write it.

But France was a Catholic country where the King supported the Catholic Church and appointed the bishops. It was dangerous to criticize the Catholic Church, especially after 1534. That year vicious written attacks on Catholic Church services were spread around, and one was found in the King's own rooms.

Calvin Leaves France

Calvin had to leave France in 1534. He traveled widely, including Italy. In 1536, in Basel in Switzerland, Calvin published a summary of his new religious ideas, *The Institutes of the Christian Religion*.

This was the most important of Calvin's writings. Calvin did not write as much as Luther, but what he wrote was always clear and well organized. Calvin kept working on the *Institutes* for many years of his life and kept publishing new editions of it.

Calvin's Ideas

In the *Institutes*, Calvin set out to give a full account of the Christian religion. He gave the book a second title: "The Basic Teaching of the Christian Religion Comprising Almost the Whole of Godliness and Whatever One Needs to Know About the Truth of Being Saved." He did not aim to make enemies, and he quoted an earlier Catholic writer, Bernard of Clairvaux (1090–1153), proving how broadminded he could be. Calvin dedicated his book, or offered it as a kind of present, to the King of France.

In the book, Calvin described God as almighty and knowing everything. God, Calvin wrote, was "infinite wisdom, justice, goodness, mercy, truth, virtue, and life." Everything that happened did so because God wanted it to. When people went to heaven or hell, that was because God wanted it so. This idea became known as **predestination**.

Calvin Comes to Geneva

When he finished his book, Calvin went back to France to finish up some family business. Then he decided to move to the German Reformation city of Strassburg, but his way to it was blocked by war. So in 1536 Calvin arrived in the town of Geneva, in what is now a part of Switzerland.

Geneva was a market town of about 7,000 people. The town had thrown out its ruling Catholic bishop and was breaking free from the rule of its overlord, the Duchy of Savoy. Geneva had decided to bring in the Reformation.

A Frenchman named Guillaume Farel (1489–1565) was trying to bring the Reformation to Geneva, but he was not as well organized as Calvin. Farel asked Calvin to help.

Calvin Expelled

Calvin soon disagreed with the council over the role of the Church in the city and was forced to leave, along with Farel. In 1538 Calvin went to Strassburg, where he was able to see how the Reformation was set up in a city run by a council. He got married in Strassburg and worked as a minister to French people in the city.

Calvin Back in Geneva

Calvin was asked to return to Geneva in 1541, and he began to work hard to bring in the Reformation and to change the town. He aimed to have more preaching and simpler church services and to have people better behaved. He had to work with the town council, but he and the council sometimes disagreed.

In 1541 the council passed Calvin's plan for running the Church in Geneva. Calvin called the priests of his Church "pastors." They joined with ordinary men who were not pastors, called "deacons", to run the church. Calvin believed that this way of running the Church came from the early Christian Church described in the Bible.

Calvin's Geneva

Calvin was a strict man. He lived a very plain, simple, hard-working life and wanted others to do the same. When he got into power in Geneva, he thought he could put his ideas about people's behavior into operation. The bars were closed and, instead, rooms were opened where people could go to read the Bible.

The Opposition to Calvin

Ami Perrin, a member of a leading family of Geneva, led people who disliked Calvin's plans. But Calvin gained a lot of respect in Geneva by upholding the Christian religion and defending it against its attackers, one of whom was a man named Michael Servetus (1511–1553), who wrote against

Christian ideas. Calvin had him put on trial, and he was executed in 1553.

Calvin Wins

Calvin was supported by many younger people and by newcomers to Geneva. In 1555 Calvin's supporters won council elections, and Perrin was driven out. Calvin was now in a much more powerful position, although he was never a dictator, or all-powerful ruler, in Geneva. Geneva had an elected government, and Calvin had to work with it. He also consulted the other pastors, who met together in a group called the Venerable Company.

SOURCE 3

I went on with my work and in the end saw that God blessed it. You pastors must also go on with your calling and maintain what I have left.

Calvin's last words to the Geneva pastors were spoken as he knew his death was approaching in 1564. They were carefully recorded by a secretary. Calvin warned the pastors not to change his system in any way.

Strict Geneva

Strict standards were kept up by a group of officials called the **Consistory**. Members could enter people's houses and look into their pans and glasses to see what they were eating and drinking, and how much. There were rules on the size of women's hats. A woman was brought before the Consistory for praying for her dead husband, as Catholics did. Dancing at weddings was banned. People had to choose their children's names from an official list.

But many people liked the high standards of behavior, which applied to everyone, rich and poor. A Scottish visitor, John Knox (1513–1572), called Calvin's Geneva "the most perfect school of Christ seen on earth since the time of the Apostles."

Calvin's Later Years

Calvin was nearly always in poor health and in pain. He died when he was only 55, worn out with hard work.

Between 1555 and his death in 1564, Calvin achieved many of his plans, including setting up the Academy in Geneva in 1559. This was a high school with a university.

The Academy increased Geneva's importance as a center to which people could come to learn Calvin's ideas and see his organization, and then go back to their own countries to try to copy them. John Knox did this in Scotland after seeing how well Geneva worked under Calvin. Calvin was deeply interested in the world outside Geneva, including such countries as Brazil and, above all, France.

Calvin's Writings

Besides the *Institutes*, Calvin produced many writings, especially studies of the Bible. He wrote many letters to rulers and politicians and to his followers, especially in France, to encourage them and keep up their spirits when they were being attacked by the Catholic Church. He believed that rulers who used their power in evil ways should be opposed.

Calvin's Influence

Calvin's influence spread very far, to countries such as the Netherlands and Scotland. It can still be seen today. In the United States, Luther's type of Christianity was brought by German and Scandinavian immigrants. In 1620 Calvin's religion was brought to New England by the **Pilgrims**, who were followers of Calvin.

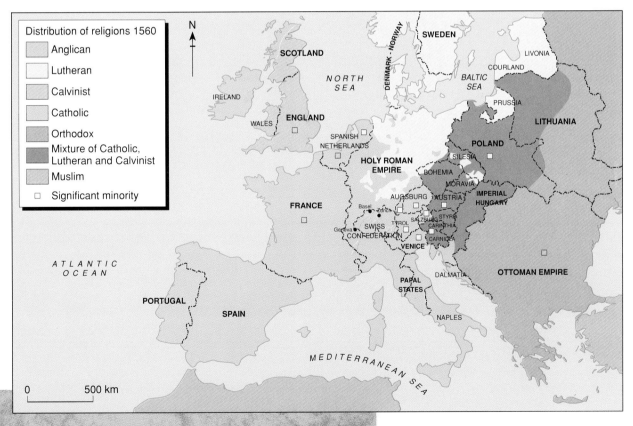

The map shows how Europe was split over religion by the time of Calvin's death.

The Reformation in England

As in other countries, the Catholic Church in England was in a bad state at the beginning of the sixteenth century. Erasmus wrote about some of the superstitions there. The leading Churchman was Cardinal Thomas Wolsey (1475–1530). His main interest was doing work for the King, Henry VIII, rather than seeing to the religious needs of ordinary Christian people.

Henry VIII and the Church

Although the state of the Catholic Church in England was poor in many ways, most English people were happy with it and with its services. Change might not have come about if the King had not decided to break free of the pope and reform religion. Henry VIII began making these changes because he wanted to divorce his first wife, Catherine of Aragon (1485–1536), so he could marry another woman. The pope refused.

In the 1530s, Henry VIII removed the Pope's power in England and became head of the Church. **Parliament** supported him. The men who brought about these changes for the King were Thomas Cromwell (1485–1540) and Thomas Cranmer (1489–1556). The monasteries were closed down. Many superstitions were ended. The Bible was printed in English.

Some good Catholics, such as Sir Thomas More (1478–1535) and Bishop John Fisher (1469–1535), did not accept the King as the head of the Church and were put to death by Henry VIII in 1535. When Henry VIII died in 1547, he was followed by a boy-King, Edward VI (1537–1553).

SOURCE 4

For the increase of virtue in Christ's religion in this kingdom of England, and to end all errors, heresies, and other abuses, it is passed by the authority of this present Parliament, that the King our sovereign lord, his heirs and followers, kings of this kingdom, shall be taken as the only supreme head on earth of the Church of England.

This is part of the Act of Supremacy of 1534, which made Henry VIII head of the Church of England. It was passed by Parliament, which is an assembly made up of the King, the Lords, and the Commons—representatives of the towns and counties. Parliament put Henry VIII's Reformation into effect in the 1530s.

This portrait of Henry VIII was painted by the German artist Hans Holbein the Younger (1497–1543) in 1536, when Henry was 45 years old.

Edward VI (reigned 1547–1553)

Henry VIII soon removed Anne Boleyn and next married Jane Seymour. They had a son, Edward VI, who was brought up in the Protestant ideas of the Reformation. When he became King, at the age of 10, Edward had people in his government who wanted to continue the Reformation along the lines of religious change in Zürich under Zwingli. Cranmer was the leader of the Church. The services were made simpler and put into English.

Mary (reigned 1553–1558)

Edward VI was ill, and he died in 1553. He was followed by his older sister, Mary, who was the daughter of Henry VIII and Catherine of Aragon. She was a Catholic. Mary tried to bring England back to the Roman Catholic Church and bring back Catholic services. She killed many people for their Protestant beliefs. Mary died in 1558 and was followed by Elizabeth.

Elizabeth (reigned 1558–1603)

Elizabeth was the daughter of Henry VIII and Anne Boleyn, and she had been brought up a Protestant. In 1559 Parliament helped her to bring in the Reformation again. The Protestant religious service was contained in the *Book of Common Prayer* (1559), and the Protestant beliefs of the Church of England were in the *Thirty-Nine Articles* (1563).

Some people did not like these changes and remained Catholic. Others, called **Puritans**, did not think the changes went far enough. But most people supported Elizabeth and her Church of England.

The Bible in English

The Bible

The Bible is the most important book for Christians to know. It is in two parts, called testaments. The first is the **Old Testament** or Hebrew Bible. It is the holy books of Jews, and Christians also believe it has important information about Jesus Christ. It was first written in Hebrew, the language of the Jews.

The second testament is the **New Testament**. It is much shorter than the Old Testament, but it contains the life of Jesus, a history of the early Christian Church, and letters from early followers of Jesus. It was first written in Greek.

Translations

Translation is putting words of one language into those of another one. A person who does this is a translator. St. Jerome (342–420) was the translator of the whole Bible into Latin, which was the main language of the Catholic Church. Jerome's translation became known as the "Vulgate."

By 1400, there were Vulgate translations in such European languages as French and German. In England, a critic of the Catholic Church, John Wyclif (1329–1384), said that the Bible would show the Church how to behave properly. His followers made an English translation of the Vulgate, but it was banned by the Church in 1407.

By the 1520s, many people felt it was time for a Bible translation into English, using books printed on presses. More English people could now read than ever before, but not many could read Latin, so they needed the Bible in English. William Tyndale (1494–1536) wanted to fill that need.

Tyndale's Translation

Tyndale said that he would make ordinary plowboys masters of the Bible. But Tyndale could not get permission to publish a Bible translation in England. He went to Germany, where he had his translation of the New Testament published in 1526. Tyndale next published a translation of parts of the Old Testament in 1530. In 1536 Tyndale was executed by Catholic rulers in the Netherlands. Sir Thomas More, a Catholic and great English scholar, said that Tyndale's translation was not worthy to be called Christ's testament, but belonged to Christ's enemy, Antichrist.

Other Versions

Before Tyndale was killed, Miles Coverdale (1488–1568) published a translation of the whole Bible in 1535. Coverdale used some of Tyndale's work. A Bible translation was published with Henry VIII's permission in 1537. In 1539, Coverdale published another version of it. This became known as "The Great Bible."

Other versions of the Bible in English were published. One of the best-known is the "King James Bible" of 1611.

SOURCE 5

A 15-year old boy came every Sunday to hear the glad and sweet news of the gospels. But when his father saw this, he angrily dragged him away and tried to make him say the Latin services with him, which made the boy very sad. Every time he went back to hear the Bible read, his father pulled him away. The boy planned to learn to read English so that he could read the New Testament for himself. Working hard, he did. Then he and his father's **apprentice** bought a copy of the New Testament, hid it under the mattress, and read it when they could.

This source, from a life of an English Protestant, William Walden, tells us that many English people longed to read the Bible and went to great expense and danger to do it. England, and many families in it, became split over religion. The boy's father nearly hanged his son for refusing to follow the Catholic religion.

*The picture is from the cover of Henry VIII's "Great Bible" of 1539. It shows King Henry giving copies of the Bible to his leading ministers, Cranmer and Cromwell. The copies are marked **verbum Dei**, meaning "the word of God." Ordinary people are given the Bible and reply "God Save the King" and Vivat Rex, meaning "Long Live the King."*

France

By 1500, the Catholic Church in France needed to be purified and reformed. Many priests and bishops were concerned mainly with money and fought off attempts to change things. But, despite **corruption** in the Church, many ordinary French people who were small farmers or peasants liked the Catholic religion, with its feasts and its many saints to pray to for help.

Ideas of Reform

Some people studied the early Church. They could see big differences between the way the Church had been then, when it was simple and pure, and the way it was in France in their own time. One of these was Jacques Lefèvre d'Étaples (1455–1536). Lefèvre studied the early Church and the writings of the apostle St. Paul. He wanted to change the Church back to the way it was at its beginning.

The King

The King was very important to religious life in France. By an agreement with the Pope, the **Concordat of Bologna** (1516), the King chose bishops and heads of monasteries in France. He gained money and power from doing this, and he wanted to keep the existing system. When Luther's ideas came into France from Germany, King Francis I (1515–1547), in 1521, ordered them to be silenced. But there were attacks on the Catholic religion in speech and writing. In 1539 and 1540, King Francis stepped up the punishment for these attacks.

King Francis I died in 1547 and was followed by his son, Henry II (1547–1559). Henry II was determined to crush the Protestants, who were known in France as **Huguenots**.

Growth of the Huguenots

Henry II set up a special court to try Huguenots. It punished over 500 people. But the Huguenots continued to grow and were supported by John Calvin in Geneva. In 1559, the Huguenots held a great national convention. The same year, Henry II was killed in an accident. He left a 15-year-old son, Francis II, to follow him.

SOURCE 6

When a vacancy arises for a bishop, the king of France shall within six months of the vacancy give to the Pope the name of a worthy man who is a suitable university graduate and over twenty-seven years of age. The Pope shall then formally appoint the person.

A concordat is an agreement or treaty between a Pope and the government of a country. The Concordat of Bologna was a treaty agreed between King Francis I and Pope Leo X in 1516. At that time, the Pope needed the help of the King of France in Italian politics.

Choosing Bishops

The Concordat of 1516 gave the King of France a free hand in appointing some of the most important people in the Church, the bishops.

By controlling the bishops, the King of France controlled the Church. Unlike other rulers, he did not have a reason to bring in the Reformation to increase his power over the Church.

But the system agreed to in the Concordat did not usually lead to good bishops being appointed. The King appointed government officials and members of noble families, to keep these important families on the side of the King.

A Power Struggle

Following Henry II's death, the Catholic Cardinal of Guise (1525–1574) took charge of the government. The Guise family was opposed by the Bourbons, who were supported by the Huguenots. The power struggle to control the King was leading into a war of religion.

Religious War

In 1560, power was now taken by Henry II's widow, Queen Catherine de' Medici (1519–1589). Catherine had the aim of avoiding civil war by giving religious rights to the Huguenots. The Guise family and Catholics challenged this policy, and in 1562 France moved into religious war. Many years of war followed.

Massacres and Assassinations

Terrible war crimes were committed by both sides. Catholics were responsible for the horrifying Massacre of St. Bartholomew's Day in 1572, when thousands of Huguenots were slaughtered, including their leader, Coligny. Later national leaders were killed, including the Cardinal of Guise and his brother the Duke in 1588, and then King Henry III in 1589.

HENRY OF NAVARRE

Henry of Navarre was born in 1553 and was brought up as a Huguenot by his mother. While a young man, he became leader of the Huguenot army in the Wars of Religion. Henry was closely related to the royal family. Following the death of King Henry III in 1589, he could claim the kingship. To win over the majority of French people, who were Catholics, he became a Catholic in 1593 and, as King Henry IV, brought peace to France in 1598. Henry gave the Huguenots religious rights in the Edict of Nantes in 1598. He became a great, peace-loving King of France, but was killed by a religious madman in 1610.

The Netherlands

The Netherlands are in northwest Europe between Germany and France. These rich lands, full of trading and industrial cities, were ruled by the Duchy of Burgundy. In the 16th century, the Duchy was taken over by Spain, whose rulers and people were strongly Catholic.

This picture is by the Huguenot artist François Dubois d'Amiens (1572). It shows the Massacre of St. Bartholomew's Day in 1572, which started in Paris and spread to other parts of France. It was the worst of the many atrocities that filled the French Wars of Religion. People regarded those who disagreed with their religious views as filth to be destroyed.

Protestants in the Netherlands

Some Netherlanders were critical of the state of the Catholic Church. The religious scholar and critic Erasmus was from the Netherlands, and his views had a strong influence on some people in the country. The Netherlands were close to Germany, and Luther's ideas also came into the country. The government cracked down hard. In 1523, two of Luther's followers were burned to death.

During the next 30 years about 2000 Netherlanders were burned to death for their religious beliefs. Some Netherlanders wanted religious changes to go further than Luther wanted. They took up the Anabaptists' ideas about getting back to the early Christian Church. Many of them were executed.

Calvinism in the Netherlands

From the 1540s on, John Calvin's religious ideas took root in the Netherlands. Nobles, middle-class people, fishermen, and skilled workers were some of those who took up Calvin's Reformation ideas. The ruler of the Netherlands, King Philip of Spain (1527-1598), tried to forbid these religious ideas, but was opposed from the 1560s on.

SOURCE 7

The image-breaking began in the western Netherlands on August 14, 1566. The weapons of the image-breakers were hatchets, hammers, ladders, and ropes. Some had guns and swords. They attacked the crosses and images that had been set up alongside the country roads, then in the villages, and finally in the cities. All the chapels, churches, and monasteries that they found shut, they broke open, destroying all the images, pictures, shrines, and other holy things that they met with.

This source about image-breaking in the Netherlands is from a Dutch history of the Reformation published in 1720 by the historian Gerard Brandt. The rich Netherlands were full of beautiful Catholic religious images. But Calvinist preachers taught people to see these as idols, which God commanded to be destroyed.

The Netherlander artist Peter Breughel the Elder (1520–1569) painted John the Baptist preaching, imagining him speaking about God to a crowd outside a Netherlands city in the 1560s. In the bottom right-hand corner of the painting, two friars are spying on John and planning to report him to the police.

Spain's Answer

King Philip was extremely angry about the image-breaking. In 1567, he sent a huge army to the Netherlands to put down religious opposition as well as criticism of his government. The army was commanded by a fierce Spanish general, the Duke of Alba (1508-1582), who increased taxes and killed many thousands of Protestants. Alba's cruel methods made people hate Spanish rule.

Resistance

From 1572 on, resistance groups took towns in the northern part of the Netherlands. They were led by William of Orange (1533–1584), who became a Calvinist. Calvinists were the greatest enemies of Spanish rule. Orange led the northern parts of the Netherlands into a new state, the United Provinces, which was independent of Spain and which supported religious toleration. From the 1580s on, Spain recovered much land in the southern part of the country under its general, Parma (1546–1592), who used less harsh methods than Alba. The Catholic faith was brought back to these areas.

WILLIAM OF ORANGE

William of Orange (1533–1584), born in Germany, was a great nobleman and the personal friend of Philip II's father, the Emperor Charles V. But he hated Alba's cruel methods and gave up his government job in 1567. Alba declared that he was a traitor. Orange became a Calvinist and led armed resistance to Spain. Under his leadership, the northern parts of the Netherlands gave up their rule by Philip II and became a new, free nation and a republic in 1581. Orange was nicknamed "the Silent." He was assassinated in 1584.

Calvinism in Europe

- Calvin's type of Christianity spread more widely than Luther's. It did not need the support of rulers to set it up. Indeed, Calvin's ideas gave courage and confidence to his followers when they fought against the ruler in the name of God.

- Yet the Netherlands did not force Calvin's ideas on the people. A founding document of the United Provinces, the Union of Utrecht (1579), laid down that "each person shall remain free in his religion and no one one shall be persecuted because of his religion."

- Like the United States later, the United Provinces had no king and formed a **federal state** based on freedom and religious toleration.

- Calvin's ideas also took strong root in Scotland, the kingdom to the north of England. In 1559–1560, John Knox (1513–1572) led nobles and the common people against the government to bring in Calvin's system.

- Calvinism also found a home in some parts of Germany.

- Important to the success of Calvinism in several parts of Europe was support from nobles, who could protect this religion on their lands. In eastern Europe, this happened in Hungary and also, for a while, in Poland.

CHAPTER

4

The Catholic Recovery

The Sack of Rome

Rome in the Renaissance

The **Renaissance** was a movement of artistic and scientific revival in the 15th and early 16th centuries. The leaders of the Renaissance aimed to recover the spirit and the achievements of ancient Greece and Rome before these cultures had become Christian. Some leaders of the Renaissance put humans, not God, at the center of their world. They honored human genius in study, music, poetry, and the arts.

Artists and writers had to make a living. They looked for patrons. A patron saw to their needs, and in return they praised and glorified the patron. This arrangement was important for rulers and other powerful patrons. Artists praised them in poetry, paintings, and statues. Rulers advertised their power by patronizing artists.

Patronage and the Popes

Italy in the Renaissance was not a united country but a group of independent states, including the one ruled by the pope in the city of Rome and central Italy. In the 15th century, the popes concentrated on ruling this state, although they also governed the Church beyond Italy. Like other rich Italian rulers, they patronized artists, who in return glorified their government. For example, the greatest Italian artist of the Renaissance, Michelangelo (1475–1564), had as his patron Pope Julius II, who reigned from 1503 to 1513. Julius gave Michelangelo the job of designing a magnificent tomb that would celebrate the pope's greatness after his death. The pope was supposed to be the representative of Christ on earth, but like other Renaissance popes, Julius was chiefly interested in money, power, and prestige.

To pay what it cost to be voted into power, popes had to make as much as they could from their position. Big building programs and lavish payments for the arts required

SOURCE 1

All the cardinals are busy with schemes and plots of their own and show little respect to God or to their positions in the Church. Bargains are made openly, and it seems these days that a refusal to make deals is regarded as undignified. They don't trade in small sums, but in thousands and ten and thousands, to the shame of the Catholic Faith and the dishonor of Almighty God. To gain the papacy, Pope Julius II has made promises without end to the cardinals, princes, barons, and to everyone that could be of any use to him in his election. He has promised them whatever they pleased to ask. He has had it in his power to give out sums of money and any number of positions in the Church.

In this source, two 16th-century Italian writers, Giustinian and Guicciardini, reported on the time just before the election of Julius II in 1503. Their accounts tell much about what was wrong with the top leadership of the Church: money was everything to them.

vast sums of money. Ordinary Christian people paid it. The indulgences sold in Germany, against which Luther protested, were used to raise money for a grand new building project to glorify the popes, St. Peter's Cathedral in Rome.

Rome was also a place of pleasure, fashion, beautiful art, music, and parties. One pope, Leo X (Pope 1513–1521), said: "God has made me pope, now let's enjoy it." The enjoyment came to a sudden end in 1527 with what became known as the Sack of Rome.

SOURCE 2

The soldiers killed at leisure. They raided the houses of the middle classes and the lesser folk, the palaces of the nobles, the convents of both sexes, and the churches. They made prisoners of men, women, and even of little children, without regard to their age or any other claim on pity. The booty they took could not be calculated, in coin, jewels, gold and silver plate, clothes, tapestries, furniture, and goods of every description.

Now, we should remember how for so many years money from throughout the Christian world has flowed into Rome, and until now has stayed there. This disaster has been an example to the whole world of how men who are so proud, so greedy for money, so murderous, so full of lust, so hypocritical, come to such an end.

This source was written by a 16th-century observer, Vettori. He recorded how the great city of Rome, capital of the popes, was raided by Spanish and German soldiers who had run amok in 1527 in the Sack of Rome. Rome had been a place of pleasure, and now it was a place of murder and rape.

Pope Leo enjoyed life, including hunting. In the painting here, the great artist Raphael (1483–1520) showed him with his nephews (1518). One of them became Pope Clement VII (Pope 1523–1534). Clement was pope during the Sack of Rome.

POPE LEO X

Leo X was pope following Julius II and reigned from 1513 to 1521. Leo came from one of Italy's ruling families, the Medici of Florence. The office of pope was being dominated by these ruling families.

This painting of **Ignatius Loyola** shows him writing his **Life**.

The Lesson

Vettori drew a lesson, which many others also took, from the Sack: God was punishing Rome for so many years of greedy and wasteful living.

Because Rome was so wrapped up in its good life, it ignored the number of people who were leaving the Catholic Church. Nothing was done to cure the abuses that caused these losses. Now things were about to change. In fact, even before the Sack of Rome, some people were beginning to return to religious values.

The Catholic Renewal

A soldier in Spain, Ignatius Loyola (1491–1556), underwent a conversion, a turning to God. He tells us about it in his *Life* (1556).

SOURCE 3

Up to my twenty-sixth year I was a man given over to the pleasures of the world and took a special delight in fighting, with a great, stupid desire to win glory. I was in a fortress which the French were attacking, where a cannon ball struck me in the leg, crushing its bones. The doctors wanted to break my leg again and reset the bones. I went through this butchery, just clenching my fist, but I got worse, showing signs of dying. My doctor said that if I was no better by midnight, I should think myself as good as dead. Yet I prayed to St. Peter, and Our Lord Jesus wished that I should get better from midnight, as I did.

Loyola goes on to tell how, in the long time it took him to get better, he read books about the life of Christ and lives of the saints and turned more and more to religion. He worked among the poor, studied at a university, became a priest, and gathered friends into what they called the Society of Jesus.

33

The Society of Jesus and the Pope

In 1539, the Society went to offer its services to the Pope, Paul III (Pope 1534–1549). Paul III was the first Pope following the Sack of Rome to be aware of the need to reform the Church. In 1540, he accepted the offer of Ignatius and his companions and officially set up the Society of Jesus.

This picture shows a bust commemorating Francis Xavier and his work.

SOURCE 4

All those who want to fight under the flag of God in our Society, which is called by the name of Jesus, and who are willing to serve only God and His representative on earth, the Pope, shall take a solemn vow and then make up their minds like this: They will be part of a group set up for this purpose; they will work in spreading the faith by preaching, by regular prayer, and by caring for others, especially teaching children and the uneducated. The members, for as long as they live, must keep it in mind every day that they serve as soldiers obeying the holy lord Pope Paul III and his successors.

This source is from Pope Paul III's order, or bull, of 1540 setting up the Society of Jesus, or Jesuits. Pope Paul III realized the value of Loyola's discipline, bravery, and obedience to the Catholic Church following the Sack of Rome.

FRANCIS XAVIER

Francis Xavier (1506-1552) was born in northern Spain in 1506, the son of a King's adviser. In 1534 he joined with Ignatius Loyola to found the Society of Jesus. He was made a priest in 1537 and was sent by the King of Portugal to preach in Portugal's colonies in Asia. Xavier arrived in Goa in India in 1542.

XAVIER'S MISSION

Xavier made large numbers of people Christians and attacked the Portuguese colonists for exploiting the local people. He traveled among the islands of the Indian Ocean. He converted the King of Sri Lanka and many of his people to Christianity. Xavier set up a Christian Church in Japan in 1548. He next prepared for a visit to China, but was exhausted by his work. He died in 1552.

Other Orders

The Jesuits formed an **order** within the Catholic Church, that is, a group of men or women carrying out particular tasks, such as preaching, teaching school, or nursing. Other new orders arose in the 16th century to meet the special needs of the time. These new orders started in Italy, where the state of the Church was worst and where war and plague caused misery for many. These orders were set up for specific reasons:

- The Barnabites were set up in the 1530s in the large Italian city of Milan, where plague victims needed care. They were founded by Antonio Maria Zaccaria, who died in 1539.

- The Capuchins were a branch of the Franciscan friars started by Matteo da Bascio (1495–1552) in Italy in the 1520s. They renewed the original ideals of the Franciscans: poverty, simplicity, and preaching.

- The Oratorians were founded by Philippo Neri (1515–1595) in about 1517 to reform life in Rome.

- The Somaschi were founded by a former soldier, Girolamo Emiliani (1480–1537) in the 1530s. They specialized in running orphanages.

- The Theatines were founded by Gian Pietro Carafa (1476–1559) and Gaetano da Thiene (1480–1547) in 1524. They aimed to improve priests and help the poor.

The Council of Trent

A council is a general assembly of the Christian Church, mostly made up of bishops. Many councils have been held during the

This painting by the great Italian artist Titian (1490–1576) shows a meeting of the Council of Trent.

Church's history. In the Middle Ages, the Council of Constance (1414–1418) met to deal with the problems of the Church. Other councils were held after 1418, but popes became suspicious of holding councils in case the council challenged the power of the pope.

The Fifth Lateran Council

This Council met in Rome between 1512 and 1517, on the eve of Luther's revolt from the Catholic Church. The Lateran Council declared that the Pope was higher than councils. It passed some reforms, but there was no sense of need for action.

Pope Paul III

Paul III was Pope from 1534 to 1549. He set up the Jesuit order. Paul asked a committee of cardinals to report on the state of the Church and accepted their frank report in 1537. He also knew that the Church's problems needed a council to solve them. Paul III invited representatives to a council in 1537. War between the main Catholic countries in Europe prevented these representatives from attending the meeting.

The Council Meets

A meeting was held in the Italian city of Trent in 1542, after the war, but was badly attended. Pope Paul III kept on trying. Late in 1545, the Council met at Trent and got to work in January 1546. One of the Pope's representatives at the Council, Cardinal Pole, addressed the members.

What the Council Achieved

- The Council of Trent set out the beliefs of the Catholic Church.

- The Council ordered bishops to stay in their bishoprics and look after the religious needs of their priests and people.

- The Council ordered training colleges, called **seminaries**, to be set up to produce well qualified, dedicated priests.

- The Council revised and standardized the worship of the Catholic Church.

SOURCE 5

The tasks of this Council are clearly set out in the Pope's letter convening us: destroying heresies; reforming church discipline and morals; and restoring the peace of the whole Church. We can perform none of these tasks alone or even together without God's help.

Before God, we, the shepherds of God's flock, must admit our blame for the ills now affecting Christ's flock. Wrong views about faith have sprung up in God's garden, the Church, which has been given to us leaders to tend. If we have not looked after this garden, we are as much the cause of the heresies as if we had taught them. As for "abuses": there is no need of an endless investigation into who is responsible—it is us!

In this source, the Pope's representative at the Council of Trent, Cardinal Pole, spoke to the delegates, mostly made up of bishops. In his frank words to the Council, Pole took up an idea from a report that he and other cardinals handed in to the Pope in 1537: this idea was that Church leaders were responsible for what was wrong. So it was now up to them to put it right.

CARDINAL REGINALD POLE

Reginald Pole (1500–1558) was born in England and was related to the royal family. In 1519, he went to Italy to study. In 1527, he came back to England but refused to agree to Henry VIII's divorce plans. He returned to Italy and joined others working to reform the Church. In 1536, Pole was linked with rebels who were against Henry's religious changes. In 1537, he was one of a group of cardinals who produced for the pope a key document on Church reform. Following his leading role in the Council of Trent, Pole returned to England in 1554 to help Queen Mary bring back Catholicism. He died there in 1558.

Missions

Christian Missions

Mission is the word used for teaching beliefs to other people. Christ told His followers to spread His message, and Christians have to try to spread their beliefs. Europe had become Christian through a long-term mission carried out by monks, priests, and friars.

Mission in Europe

In the 16th century, the Catholic Church went on with its mission in Europe. It did this in two ways:

- In parts of Europe that had left the Catholic Church, strong efforts were made by Catholics to win people back. The best example of this was in England. Englishmen were trained abroad to be priests, and from 1574 on, they went back home to bring English people back to Catholicism. This was a crime in England, and many of these priests were executed between 1577 and 1681.

- The Catholic Church continued to try to teach people within the Catholic parts of Europe, such as France. Priests and bishops worked to make peasants more sober and harder working and to make them follow the teachings of the Church about sexual relations and marriage.

Missions Overseas

The Reformation and the Catholic reply to it happened at a time when Europeans were finding out more about the world beyond Europe than ever before. Europeans quickly conquered huge areas of the world in America and also in parts of Asia, such as the Philippines. The two leading conquering countries, Spain and Portugal, were firmly Catholic. They sent priests, friars, and Jesuits to make the world Catholic. These missionaries needed to find out as much as they could about countries that were new to them. Francis Xavier was the model for all Catholic missionaries.

SOURCE 6

The people we have met so far are the best who have yet been discovered, and it seems to me that we shall never find among non-Christians a race to equal the Japanese. They are a people of very good manners. They prize honor above all else in the world—much more than riches. They are very courteous in their dealings with one another. They are very fond of hearing about things of God, chiefly when they understand them. They like to hear things argued according to reason. This land of Japan is very fit for our holy faith to increase in greatly; and if we knew how to speak the language, I have no doubt whatsoever that we would make many Christians.

This source is from a letter that Xavier sent to the Jesuits in Goa, India, in November 1540, describing Japan.

Francis Xavier was very hopeful about making Japan Catholic. For about 100 years after his visit, the Catholic Church in Japan grew, but it was then attacked and driven underground. Many non-Europeans feared that if they became Catholic, their own culture would be overwhelmed by that of the missionaries. In China, which had a rich civilization, the Italian Jesuit Matteo Ricci (1552–1610) worked to bring together Chinese culture and the Catholic religion. He became highly skilled in the Chinese language.

Francis Xavier also knew that he had to learn Japanese to succeed. He tried to understand the Japanese and not to patronize them. But he saw them through his own eyes and thought that they had the values of his own class and country, especially what he called "honor."

Missionaries often tried to protect native peoples from being abused by colonists. A friar, Bartolomé de las Casas (1474–1566), accused colonists in South America of genocide, the murder of an entire people, against native Americans. Native peoples in America often saw missionaries as agents of colonization and attacked them.

The Missions and the Map

Outside of Europe, the conquerors and the missionaries thought the world was "new" and that they had to name it. Sometimes they named places for European rulers. The Spanish named the Philippines for King Philip of Spain, and the French named Louisiana for King Louis of France and New Orleans for his brother, the Duke of Orléans. But mostly, the missionaries wanted to put the stamp of the Catholic faith on the map.

This map shows how the Jesuits organized their mission along the Chesapeake Bay.

In 1549, Friar Luís and other companions were sent to Tampa Bay. They said they would make that land peaceful, convert the people to Christianity, and bring them to serve and obey the Spanish government. They would do this by words alone. The friar then set out at the king's expense in 1549. He went on shore with four other friars whom he had brought with him and some unarmed sailors—because this was the way they had to begin preaching. Many of the native people of Florida came down to the shoreline and, without listening to a single word, clubbed Friar Luís to death, with one or two companions. Then they ate them.

This source is from an account, by the historian Gomera, of the Friar Luís Cancer de Barbustro's attempts to convert the Native Americans of Florida peacefully. It shows how missionary work was viewed by those in power as a way of enslaving the Native Americans. The French conquered large parts of North America. In Canada the local tribes fought back, and large numbers of Jesuits were killed.

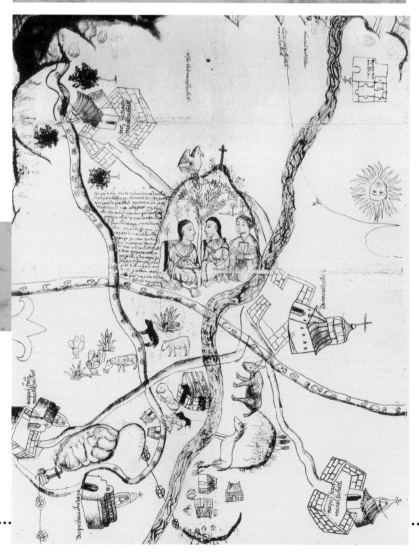

In the Caribbean, they named Trinidad for the "Blessed Trinity" of God the Father, the Son, and the Holy Spirit. They named Santo Domingo for the founder of the Dominican friars, St. Dominic. Santiago de Cuba was named in honor of the saint of Spain, St. James.

In South America, they named Saõ Paulo, Brazil, for St. Paul and Rosario, Argentina, for a favorite prayer, the rosary. In Mexico, they named Vera Cruz in honor of the "true cross" of Christ.

When the missionaries came up into New Mexico, Texas, and California, they usually named a place in honor of the special feast day on which they arrived: Corpus Christi ("body of Christ"), Texas, and Santa Barbara (St. Barbara), San Francisco (St. Francis), and San Diego (St. James), California. Sometimes they named a place for a special devotion: Santa Fé ("holy faith"), New Mexico, or Sacramento ("the holy sacrament"), California. When they wanted to honor Christ's mother, Mary, the missionaries called a little settlement in California "the village of Our Lady Mary, Queen of the Angels." Today, we know it as Los Angeles.

The French in America also put their Catholic religion on the map. Des Moines, Iowa, means "monks", and the French missionaries honored St. Paul when they named a little camp in Minnesota for him.

The Index and the Inquisition

Books
In the Middle Ages, books were expensive to produce. They were copied out by hand on to expensive pages made from treated animal skins. Few people could read or have access to books.

In the middle of the 15th century, all of this changed. Printing was invented in Germany and spread fast across Europe. Books could be produced in multiple copies. The very large books, such as Bibles, were still quite expensive. But now, inexpensive booklets, pamphlets, and sheets could be mass produced for the equivalent of a few pennies. More and more people were going to school and learning to read. Protestants like Luther made very good use of the inexpensive presses to weaken the power of Catholicism.

The Catholic Reply
How was the Catholic Church to deal with this threat? There were two ways: to explain its views in writing as well as the Protestants did, or to ban their books. At that time, no Catholic writer could write for the general public as well as Luther could explain Protestant views; he could write like a very good modern newspaper journalist. The Church chose to ban books that were against Catholicism in any way.

Banning Books
Various attempts were made by governments to ban anti-Catholic books. In England in 1530 and 1531, when King Henry VIII was still on the side of the Pope, long lists of banned books, including Bibles in English, were drawn up. In 1550, the Emperor Charles V banned books by Luther, Zwingli, Bucer, and Calvin. In 1559, Pope Pius IV issued an *Index of Prohibited Books*, to be regularly kept up to date.

Pornographic books were put on the Index. Books on the Index sold so well that some writers paid bribes to get their books put on.

The Inquisition
In the Middle Ages, the Catholic Church was often criticized by those it called heretics. The Inquisition was set up to inquire into the beliefs of these heretics and either make them give up their beliefs or hand them over to the government to be burned.

SOURCE 8

Rule I

All books which were condemned prior to 1515 by Popes or Councils, and are not listed in this Index, are to stand condemned in the original way.

Rule II

Books of leading heretics—those who have made up or encouraged heresy since 1515 or who have been or still are heads and leaders of heretics, such as Luther, Zwingli, Calvin, and the like—whatever their names, titles, or lines of argument—are banned without exception. Translations of books of the Old Testament may be allowed by the judgment of bishops for the use of well-educated and highly religious men only. If the reading of the Holy Bible in the ordinary language of the people is allowed without restriction, more losses than gains will result. Bishops, taking the advice of local priests, **may** allow Catholic translations of the Bible to be read by people whose religion will not, in the opinion of these authorities, be damaged by the reading. Books in the language of the ordinary people dealing with arguments between Catholics and Protestants are not to be widely available.

*This source is from the **Index of Pope Pius IV**, dated 1559 and also known as the **Index of the Council of Trent**. The Index shows that the leaders of the Catholic Church were sometimes afraid of the people and unwilling to trust them with the Bible in their own language or with reading arguments between Catholics and Protestants.*

The Inquisition was started up again in Spain in 1481. It was to investigate Jews who had become Christians and were suspected of not really believing in the Catholic faith. It was also revived in Italy in 1542 to keep Protestant ideas out of the country. In Spain and its empire, the Inquisition was part of the state. It slaughtered many thousands of people.

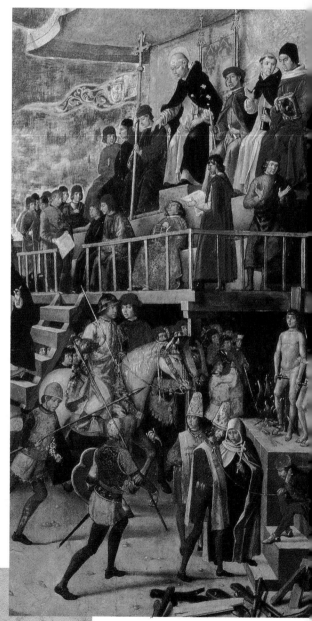

*An **auto da fé**, or public burning of heretics, painted by the 16th-century Spanish artist Pedro Berreguete.*

Conclusion

The extent of the Catholic Recovery

The Catholic Church in a Troubled Time

In 1540, it would have been easy to write off the Catholic Church. Large parts of Europe had left the Catholic Church: England, huge areas of Germany, many parts of Switzerland, and all of Scandinavia. Luther was still active. Calvin had written his clear summary of Protestant beliefs, the *Institutes of the Christian Religion*, in 1536. Protestant ideas were spreading in France and the Netherlands. The Council of Trent had not yet met. The Jesuits were a tiny group, not known outside Rome. It looked as if the Catholic Church might survive only in Italy, Spain, and Portugal.

Recovery

Only 100 years later, the situation was much altered. The Protestant challenge had been fought off. The Catholic religion had come back strongly in some German-speaking parts of Europe, such as Bavaria and Austria. Protestantism stopped expanding in Europe.

How had this unexpected recovery, or **Counter Reformation**, come about?

- Better, holy popes, like Pius V (Pope 1566–1572)
- Dedicated bishops, like Carlo Borromeo (1538–1584), raising standards in their bishoprics
- Good, well-trained priests, coming out of seminaries
- Brilliant preaching and schooling by the Jesuits
- Use of art, music, and architecture to make churches attractive to people.

At the height of the Counter Reformation, the Italian artist Gian Lorenzo Bernini (1598–1680) added a colonnade, or row of columns, in front of the Catholic Church's main church building, St. Peter's in Rome. The colonnade forms arms to symbolize how the Catholic Church aimed to embrace the world in its arms.

The building of St. Peter's had triggered trouble for the Church. To raise the money for it, indulgences had been sold in Germany, sparking Martin Luther's protest. One hundred years later, as St. Peter's was completed, the Catholic Church had put many of its troubles behind it.

SOURCE 1

So I began to meditate on the place in hell which I deserved for my sins, and I gave great praises to God, for my life was so changed that I seemed not to recognize my own soul. While I was meditating in this way, a strong movement seized me without my realizing why. It seemed as if my soul were about to leave my body, because it could no longer hold itself in and could not wait for such a great blessing.

This source is from the Life—the autobiography—of the Spanish saint, Teresa of Ávila (1515–1582). Teresa was a mystic—a person who meditates, or thinks very deeply about God, and has visions and spiritual experiences that cannot be explained. The mystic believes that these experiences come straight from God. Teresa was also a great organizer. She reorganized and reformed her order of nuns. Teresa was the greatest woman of the Counter-Reformation.

Canonizations

Teresa of Ávila was officially made a saint, or **canonized**, in 1622. The canonizations that took place in that year were splendid ceremonies, held in St. Peter's. They allowed the Catholic Church to mark its recovery. Those canonized included other Spanish people, Ignatius Loyola and Francis Xavier.

This recognized the great importance of the Spanish in the recovery of the Catholic Church.

POPE PIUS V

Pius V (Pope 1566–1572) was a complete contrast to the earlier popes of the Renaissance period who had put their own interests, pleasures, and families before the needs of the Church. Unlike several popes of the Renaissance, he did not come from a princely or noble family; his background was lowly. He entered the Dominican order and became a bishop. His rule also shows the ruthless side of the Counter-Reformation; he was head of the Inquisition in the northern Italian territory of Lombardy. He was also a friend of Carlo Borromeo, who became bishop of Milan.

CARLO BORROMEO

As a young man, Carlo Borromeo (1538–1584) took part in the Council of Trent. In 1563, he took over as bishop of the huge bishopric of Milan. He brought in the changes ordered by the Council of Trent and became a model of what the new-style bishops of the Catholic Church were to be. Borromeo lived very simply and cared for the poor of Milan, especially in an outbreak of plague in 1576. He gave special attention to education and opened Sunday schools to teach people religion, as well as seminaries to train priests.

The Reformation and its Effects

Tragedy

There were some bad effects of the Reformation. These were:

- War: religious division led to war. The Wars of Religion in France from 1562 to 1598 were savage and long. Thousands were massacred. Across Europe, a war in the name of religion, the Thirty Years War, raged from 1618 to 1648. It left much of Germany devastated.

- Division: Christ said His followers should be united. The Reformation made them more divided. Christians today try to repair the division and the damage done in the Reformation.

Benefits

Although the harm caused by the Reformation should be remembered, so should its good effects:

- Renewal. Leaders of the Reformation, such as Luther and Calvin, tried to bring the Christian Church back to its origin. They restated basic ideas, especially that Christ saves and that the Bible is central. Their movements helped activate the Catholic Church to reform its own ways.

- Freedom. Luther bravely stood up for the right of the individual to speak up and to be true to his or her conscience. Calvin denounced tyrants.

- Progress. Some writers stress how Protestant ideas helped lead to economic and scientific development.

- Toleration. Differences of religious beliefs in countries such as the Netherlands and England following the Reformation brought about the need to recognize people's right to differ.

SOURCE 2

There are many rulers these days, calling themselves Christians, who arrogantly assume that their power is unlimited, over which even God has no control. They have plenty of flatterers who adore them as if they were gods on earth. Others, either through fear or force, seem to believe that rulers should be obeyed in everything, by everyone. Rulers go beyond their limits, not happy with the proper authority which almighty God has given them, but always trying to take the power over human beings that God has kept to Himself. Not happy to demand the bodies and goods of their subjects at their whim, they claim also to force people's consciences, which belong only to Jesus Christ.

Kings Are Made by the People

The people establish kings and with their support confirm the choice of kings. They have their power and rule from the people. They are of the same material as other people, raised from the earth by the voice of the people.

The Whole Body of the People is Above the King

Seeing that the people choose and establish their kings, it follows that the whole body of the people is above the king, since it is obvious that someone who is set up by another is under the person who has put him there. The person who receives his power from another is in fact less than the one from whom he gets his authority.

*This source is from an anonymous French Huguenot work of 1579, **Vindiciae Contra Tyrannos, A Defense of Liberty Against Tyrants**. It laid down principles that are at the heart of modern democracy. Some were adopted in the United States Constitution: that state power is not absolute; that rulers have their power from the people and are the servants, not the masters, of the people.*

Why Did People Accept the Reformation?

- Many people were forced into accepting religious change. Powerful rulers such as Henry VIII and Gustavus Vasa imposed change on their subjects. Other people accepted religious change out of respect and loyalty to their ruler, who was bringing in the Reformation.

- Some people accepted the Reformation for financial reasons. The Catholic Church was expensive to support, and many hoped for lower church taxes and payments. In England, when the monasteries were closed down, their lands were sold off to the nobles and to wealthy people. Many families benefited from this change.

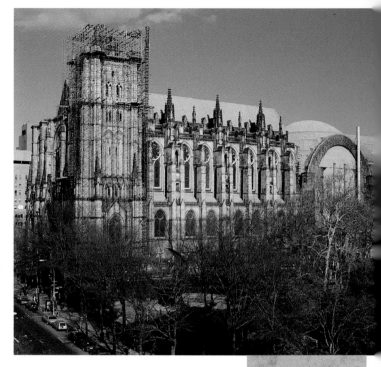

St John's Episcopalian Cathedral in Manhattan, New York.

- Rulers sometimes introduced the Reformation in order to get their hands on the wealth of the Church, defy the pope, and control the Church. This was important because the Church was the chief means of education and information.

- Some people took up religious change for reasons of nationalism. They hated a Church controlled from far away, in Rome.

- None of these reasons fully explain why the Reformation had such appeal. The real reasons for accepting it were religious. People were anxious about the fate of their souls. The teachings of Luther and Calvin gave them reassurance. The Reformation was a great religious experience.

The Reformation Today

Is the Reformation alive today? In most countries of Europe, where the Reformation and the Catholic reply to it started, church attendance is very low. Writers speak of de-Christianization, meaning large numbers of people leaving the Christian Church.

Yet outside Europe, which for many centuries was the only Christian continent, Christianity has grown, for example in Africa. In the 16th century, the Church of England was a tiny, breakaway Church, with just a few million members. Today it is a worldwide Church, the **Anglican** or **Episcopalian** Church. Other Protestant churches have also grown, and some of them have worldwide membership.

In the United States, attendance at church is much higher than it is in Europe. The church in the picture is the huge Episcopalian Cathedral of St. John in New York City—a church of the Reformation.

Time Line

1483	Martin Luther is born.
1491	Henry VIII of England, Menno Simmons, and Ignatius Loyola are born.
1505	Martin Luther becomes a monk.
1509	John Calvin is born.
1512–1515	Catholic Church's Fifth Lateran Council.
1516	Concordat of Bologna between Pope Leo X and King Francis I of France.
1517	Luther issues his *Ninety-Five Theses* against indulgences.
1520	Pope Leo X expels Luther from the Church.
1521	Luther appears at the the Diet of Worms and refuses to change his beliefs.
1522	Beginning of Reformation in Denmark.
1523	Beginning of Reformation in Zürich.
1525	Peasants' Revolt in Germany; Luther writes *Against the Murdering, Thieving Hordes of Peasants*; first adult baptisms in Zürich.
1526	William Tyndale's English translation of the New Testament is published.
1527	Sack of Rome; beginnings of Reformation in Sweden.
1529	Tyndale's Old Testament in English published; fall of Cardinal Wolsey; Henry VIII calls the Reformation Parliament.
1534	Act of Supremacy makes Henry VIII head of the Church of England.
1535	Miles Coverdale publishes the entire Bible in English; radical Anabaptist revolution in Münster.
1536	Calvin publishes *The Institutes of the Christian Religion*.
1536–1539	Monasteries closed down in England.
1537	Report of Catholic Church leaders on reform of the Church.
1539	The "Great Bible" published in English.
1540	Pope Paul III sets up the Jesuit order.
1541	Calvin established in Geneva.
1542	Inquisition set up in Italy.
1545	Council of Trent meets.
1546	Death of Luther.
1547	Death of Henry VIII; Protestant Edward VI becomes King of England.
1553	King Edward VI dies; Mary, a Catholic, becomes Queen of England.
1555	Peace of Augsburg in Germany.
1558	Death of Queen Mary; Elizabeth, a Protestant, becomes Queen of England.
1559	Reformation brought back to England; Calvin founds Geneva Academy; national convention of Huguenots; Pope Pius II issues *Index of Prohibited Books*.
1559–1560	John Knox brings Reformation to Scotland.
1562	Wars of Religion in France.
1563	Council of Trent ends.
1564	Death of Calvin.
1572	Resistance to Spain begins to succeed in the Netherlands; Massacre of St. Bartholomew's Day in France.
1593	Huguenot leader Henry of Navarre becomes Catholic and King of France.
1598	Edict of Nantes brings peace to France.
1611	King James Bible is published.

Glossary

Amish Peaceful **Anabaptist** groups.

Anabaptists People who believed that the **Reformation** of Luther and Zwingli did not go far enough. They practiced baptism of adult believers only, as in the early Church.

Anglican Of the Church of England.

anticlericalism Hatred of priests and Church leaders.

apprentice A live-in young worker learning his or her job from a skilled person.

baptism The ceremony of baptizing someone.

baptize To sprinkle or wash a person with water as a sign that the person is a Christian and a member of the Church.

bishopric The district governed by a bishop.

bull A solemn document from a pope.

canonized Officially placed on the list of saints.

cardinal A Church leader under the pope; the cardinals elect the pope.

civic reformers **Protestant** leaders who brought the **Reformation** into individual cities, with the support of city councils.

Concordat of Bologna An agreement (1516) between the Pope and the King of France to allow the King to name the bishops in France.

confession A religious act in which people tell their sins to their priest to receive forgiveness.

consistory A body set up in Geneva under Calvin to regulate people's behavior.

converted Changed from one religion to another, or had a deep religious experience that strengthened one's own faith.

corruption Dishonesty, evil, bribery.

Counter-Reformation The improvement and renewal in the Catholic Church that took place after the **Reformation**.

Episcopalian A member of a Church governed by, or belonging to, bishops.

friar A religious man who lives a poor, simple life and preaches to people about Christ.

heresy The act of disbelieving and attacking the beliefs of the Church. Someone who did this was a heretic.

Huguenots French **Protestants**.

Humanist Someone who studied the ancient writings of Greece and Rome. Christian Humanists studied early Christian writings and the Bible in its original languages.

Hutterites A peaceful **Anabaptist** group.

image-breaking Destruction of Catholic religious images by Calvinists, who saw them as idols that God commanded to be destroyed.

indulgence A release from punishment for sins, given by the Church.

Jesuits Members of the Society of Jesus, set up by the Pope in 1540.

manifesto A public declaration of principles and policy.

monk A religious man who lives with others in a monastery, praying, working, and living simply.

New Testament The second part of the Bible, containing the gospels, or life stories of Christ, with other important early Christian writings.

Old Testament The first part of the Bible, dealing with the covenant made by God with Moses.

order A group in the Catholic Church of priests, brothers, friars, monks, or nuns.

Parliament The English national assembly of the King or Queen, the Lords, and elected representatives that meets to pass laws.

Pilgrims The **Puritans** who sailed in the "Mayflower" and founded Plymouth, Massachusetts in 1620.

predestination The belief that God has decided in advance all those who are going to be saved in heaven or damned in hell.

Protestant Someone who gave up the Catholic Church and took up the **Reformation**; later, anyone who was a member of one of the Protestant churches.

Purgatory A place where most people were believed to go after they died, to spend some time being purified of their sins.

Puritan An English **Protestant** who believed the **Reformation** in England had not gone far enough and should be taken further.

Reformation The huge breakaway movement from the Catholic Church in the 16th century, which created new **Protestant** Churches.

Renaissance A movement that began in Italy in the 14th and 15th centuries, attempting to recover the culture of ancient Greece and Rome.

siege An attempt to take control of a town or fort by keeping it surrounded by an armed force.

seminaries Training colleges for priests, originally set up by the Council of Trent.

simony Selling holy objects or positions in the Church for money.

Index